242.62   "My First Book of
             Bible Devotions"
          David C. Cook Publishing

DATE DUE

My First Book of Bible Devotions

Is Presented To

_____

On

_____

By

_____

◆

"*L*ove the Lord your God with all your heart and with all your soul and with all your mind and with all your strength."

MARK 12:30

◆ My First Book of Bible Devotions ◆

Chariot Books
A Division of Cook Communications

Chariot Books™ is an imprint of Chariot Family Publishing
Cook Communications, Colorado Springs, Colorado 80918
Cook Communications, Paris, Ontario
Kingsway Communications, Eastbourne, England

MY FIRST BOOK OF BIBLE DEVOTIONS
© 1981, 1982, 1985, 1986, 1987, 1988, 1989, 1991 by David C. Cook Publishing Co.

Cover illustration by Richard Hook
Cover and interior design by Dawn Lauck
Edited by Julie Smith

First printing, 1991
Printed in Singapore
99 98 97 96 95   8 7 6 5 4

Library of Congress Cataloging-in-Publication Data

My first book of Bible devotions.
          p.   cm.
Summary: Combining Bible stories about Jesus with stories illustrating how they apply to children's everyday lives.
ISBN 1-55513-416-5
1. Bible Stories, English—N.T. 2. Children's stories—America. 3. Children—Prayer-books and devotions—English. [1. Bible stories—N.T. 2. Prayer books and devotions.]
BS2401.M92 1991
242'.62—dc20

                                                                           90-37714
                                                                              CIP
                                                                               AC

DEAR PARENTS,

Each Bible story in *My First Book of Bible Devotions* is followed by a story about Brenda, Michael, or their friends. Each pair of stories focuses on the same theme, repeating the Scripture passage and Verse to Remember.

Why pair Bible stories and "everyday" application stories in a devotional book? The repetition of the theme and verse will help children remember them. And, as they recall the "everyday" stories, they'll be eager to apply the Bible's teaching to their lives—just as the children in the story have done.

In addition, following each everyday story there's a suggestion to help you incorporate the Bible teaching into your family's daily life—as you play or work or worship together.

CONTENTS

The Angel Tells About Jesus
LUKE 1:26-38, 46-55

God chose Mary to be the mother of the most special baby ever born. The baby would be God's very own Son. God sent the angel Gabriel to tell Mary the news.

Mary was surprised to see an angel. She was a little afraid, too.

"Mary," said Gabriel. "Don't be afraid. God has chosen you to be the mother of a special baby boy. His name will be Jesus. Your baby will be the Son of God." Then the angel left.

Mary was very happy about this wonderful news.

PRAYER
Dear God, I am happy You gave Mary such a special baby boy—Your Son!

A BIBLE VERSE TO REMEMBER
The Father has sent his Son to be the Savior of the world.   I JOHN 4:14B

Brenda's Good News Day
LUKE 1:26-38, 46-55

Brenda practiced saying her Bible verse while Mother pinned her angel costume.

Brenda's sister Susan hung up the phone. "Good news! Aunt Jill and Uncle Dave can come for Christmas."

Brenda's brother Jeff came running in with the mail and said, "Guess what! I got a Christmas card from my friend."

Brenda said, "I didn't get a phone call or card."

Mother smiled and said, "But you have the best news of all. It's in your Bible verse that tells why we have Christmas."

And Brenda said, "The Father has sent his Son to be the Savior of the world."

PRAYER
Dear God, thank You for the best news of all—that Your
Son Jesus is the reason we have Christmas!

A BIBLE VERSE TO REMEMBER

The Father has sent his Son to be the Savior of the world.

I JOHN 4:14B

PARENTS: Remind your child that Mary heard special good news from an angel. Play a simple game by asking, "What did the angel tell Mary?" Help your child answer, "Jesus is coming!" That is the best news of all.

A Beautiful Baby
LUKE 2:1-7

Mary and her husband, Joseph, had to go to Bethlehem. When they got there, Joseph looked everywhere for a room, but the only place he could find was a stable where animals lived.

"I don't mind staying in the stable," Mary said.

Soon after that baby Jesus was born. Mary wrapped Him in soft cloth. Then she looked around. What could she use for her baby's bed? She saw a manger, a box filled with hay. Very gently, she laid baby Jesus in the manger.

"Look at baby Jesus. Isn't He beautiful?" said Mary.

Joseph smiled. "Yes, He is a fine baby. He is God's own Son. We will take good care of Him."

PRAYER
Dear Jesus, thank You for coming to earth as a tiny, little baby.

A BIBLE VERSE TO REMEMBER

For God so loved the world that he gave his one and only Son, that whoever believes in him shall not perish but have eternal life.

JOHN 3:16

The Christmas Birthday Cake
LUKE 2:1-7

Brenda's mother baked cakes for lots of people at Christmas. She showed Brenda and Dad and Susan the cakes she had made. She said, "Now I am making a cake for our family. What words should I put on it?"

Susan said, "It could be like the one that says *Merry Christmas.*"
Mother said, "But Christmas is when we celebrate Jesus' birthday."
Dad said, "Our cake could say *Happy Birthday, Jesus!*"
Brenda nodded. *"Happy Birthday, Jesus!"*

PRAYER
Happy birthday, Jesus! I love You!

A BIBLE VERSE TO REMEMBER

For God so loved the world that he gave his one and only Son, that whoever believes in him shall not perish but have eternal life.

JOHN 3:16

PARENTS: If you and your child see a baby this week, point out some of the things a baby does. Mention that baby Jesus slept, cried, and wanted to be held like all babies. Remind your child of birthdays in your family and associate the Christmas celebration with Jesus' birthday.

Shepherds Hear the Good News
LUKE 2:8-20

One night some shepherds sat in a field and watched their sheep. Suddenly they saw an angel. How surprised and scared those shepherds were!

The angel said, "Don't be afraid! I came to tell you some happy, happy news! Tonight God gave a special gift to all people everywhere. His own Son, Jesus, has just been born. You will find Him wrapped in cloth and lying in a manger."

Then more angels came. "Praise to God in heaven," they said.

Soon the angels went back to heaven. The shepherds ran to Bethlehem as fast as their legs would carry them. There they found Mary and Joseph, and baby Jesus was lying in the manger, just as the angel had promised.

The shepherds were very happy. They thanked God for sending His Son.

PRAYER
Dear Lord Jesus, I wish I could have run to Bethlehem with
the shepherds to see You.

A BIBLE VERSE TO REMEMBER
But the angel said to them, "Do not be afraid. I bring you good news of great joy that will be for all the people." LUKE 2:10

The Angel Song
LUKE 2:8-20

Carlos and his mother were driving to church. "Away in a manger," sang Carlos.

"That sounds very nice," said Mother. "Be sure to sing loud at the Christmas program so we can hear the song about Jesus. You have a special song for the people at church just like the angels had for the shepherds."

At church Carlos saw lots of people. At first he was a little scared, but then he remembered that the people wanted to hear the song about baby Jesus. So when his class started to sing, Carlos sang loud and clear, just like the angels did for the shepherds.

PRAYER
Dear God, help me to tell people about Jesus, just like the
angels did.

A BIBLE VERSE TO REMEMBER

But the angel said to them, "Do not be afraid. I bring you good news of great joy that will be for all the people."

LUKE 2:10

PARENTS: Help your child think of people he can tell the good news about Jesus' birth. Perhaps your child knows a song about Jesus that he would like to sing as one way to tell others about Jesus.

God Watches Over Jesus
MATTHEW 2:1-23

Some wise men followed a bright, beautiful star. They were going to see the baby who would be a king someday. That baby was Jesus.

King Herod didn't want a new king. He wanted to keep on being king himself. He wanted the wise men to tell him where to find the baby.

But after the wise men saw Jesus, they didn't tell Herod where Jesus was. God had told them in a dream that Herod wanted to hurt Jesus.

Joseph had a dream, too. An angel told him to leave Bethlehem quickly. "Take the baby to a place where He will be safe," the angel said.

Mary and Joseph left their home and went far away so Jesus would be safe. After a long time, an angel told Joseph in a dream, "You can take the baby home now." The king had died, so he couldn't hurt baby Jesus.

Mary and Joseph were happy. They could take Jesus home at last.

PRAYER
Thank You, God, for keeping baby Jesus safe and for keeping me safe.

*A BIBLE VERSE
TO REMEMBER
But if you trust
the Lord, you
will be safe.*
PROVERBS 29:25B
(ICB)

Carlos and Angie
MATTHEW 2:1-23

Carlos and his baby sister Angie were in the car. Carlos waved at Mother as she filled the car with gas. Then he looked at Angie. She sounded as if she might cry.

Carlos said, "Where is your toy dog, Bow-wow? He will make you smile." Carlos found Bow-wow in Angie's blanket. He gave Angie the dog and she smiled.

When Mother got into the car, Carlos said, "Angie was sad, but I took care of her. I found Bow-wow."

Mother said, "You must have remembered the story about Jesus. His family took care of Him, too."

Carlos said, "I'm glad I can help take care of Angie. And I'm glad Jesus' family took care of Him."

PRAYER
Dear God, I'm glad I have a family that takes care of me.
Thank You for my family.

A BIBLE VERSE TO REMEMBER

But if you trust the Lord, you will be safe.

PROVERBS 29:25B (ICB)

PARENTS: Talk with your child about how God uses you to keep him safe. In what ways does your child help care for others, as Carlos cared for Angie? Together, act out some ways you protect your child, such as holding hands and looking both ways before crossing a street.

Jesus Goes to a Wedding
JOHN 2:1-11

Jesus and His friends were invited to a wedding party. Jesus' mother was at the party, too.

The bride and groom and all their friends were having a good time. There was lots of good food to eat. But something happened. Soon, there was nothing to drink. The wine was all gone.

Jesus' mother said to Him, "Can You help?" She told the servants, "Do whatever Jesus tells you to."

Jesus told the servants to fill some big jars with water. When the jars were full, Jesus said, "Now, dip some water out and take it to the man in charge of the party."

The man in charge tasted the water. "How good this is!" he said to the servants. "You have saved the best wine until now."

Jesus had turned the water into wine. Jesus' friends thought, *Isn't it wonderful what Jesus can do?*

PRAYER
Dear Jesus, it is wonderful what You can do!

A BIBLE VERSE TO REMEMBER

Sing to him, sing praise to him; tell of all his wonderful acts.

PSALM 105:2

Michael the Helper
JOHN 2:1-11

Michael heard a story about Jesus helping people. He wanted to be a helper, too.

One day Michael went to Mrs. Ferguson's house. Mrs Ferguson told Michael, "Our guinea pig, Sam, got out this morning. He is sleeping under the sofa."

"Sam is sleepy, just like I was," said Michael. "But I woke up when I smelled breakfast."

Mrs. Ferguson, said, "What a good idea. Sam likes lettuce for breakfast. I'll get some."

Michael held the lettuce under the sofa, and Sam ran over to it. Mrs. Ferguson put him back in his cage.

"You were a good helper, Michael. You made Jesus happy by helping me," said Mrs. Ferguson. "I think Sam is happy, too."

PRAYER
Dear Jesus, I want to help people, too, and make You happy.

A BIBLE VERSE TO REMEMBER

Sing to him, sing praise to him; tell of all his wonderful acts.
PSALM 105:2

PARENTS: This week let your child know you need his help—even with things like putting the spoons on the table or throwing away trash. Praise your child often for helping.

Jesus Teaches People to Worship

LUKE 4:14-22

One day Jesus visited the town where He grew up. He went to God's house with all the other people to worship God. The men took turns reading from a Bible scroll, a long, rolled-up paper with God's words.

When it was Jesus' turn, He read, "God sent Me to tell people about God. He sent me to help people." Jesus said, "The words I read are about Me. I am the one God has sent to help and teach you."

Jesus loved the people and wanted them to learn about God.

PRAYER
I love to learn about You, God. Thank You for people who teach me about You.

A BIBLE VERSE TO REMEMBER
Come, let us bow down in worship, let us kneel before the Lord our Maker.
PSALM 95:6

Making Music for God
LUKE 4:14-22

It was Carlos's birthday. He brought his new drum to Sunday school. Miss Karen said, "I brought my guitar. Let's play together and sing."

Everyone played instruments or clapped as they sang, "Worship God today. Worship with a song. Joyfully, joyfully. Joyfully, joyfully. Worship with a song."*

At the end of the song, Miss Karen said, "We sounded great. Let's show God how much we love Him by doing our song again." And the whole class showed love to God.

Sing to the tune of "Row, Row, Row Your Boat."

PRAYER
Dear God, I love to go to Your house and sing songs to You.

A BIBLE VERSE TO REMEMBER

Come, let us bow down in worship, let us kneel before the Lord our Maker.   PSALM 95:6

PARENTS: Provide some homemade rhythm instruments such as an oatmeal-box drum, wooden spoons, or a cardboard-tube trumpet. Then play and sing familiar songs about Jesus as part of your family worship.

God Takes Care of Us
MATTHEW 6:25-34

Jesus knew the people He was talking to were worried. They worried, "What if I don't have food to eat or clothes to wear? What if something happens to my house and I don't have a place to sleep?"

He didn't want them to worry. Jesus looked at the sky and saw a little bird. He said, "Look at that bird. Birds don't worry about their food. God takes care of them. And God loves you more than birds."

He saw a pretty flower. Jesus said, "Look at that flower. Flowers don't worry about their clothes or houses. God takes care of them, and God loves you more than flowers!"

The people knew Jesus was right. If God took such good care of birds and flowers, they could be sure God would take care of them, too.

PRAYER
Thank You, God, for Your promise to take care of me.

A BIBLE VERSE TO REMEMBER
My God will meet all your needs according to his glorious riches in
Christ Jesus.   PHILIPPIANS 4:19

The New Room
MATTHEW 6:25-34

Brenda was visiting Aunt Jill and Uncle Dave. Aunt Jill said, "Your daddy is fixing up a new room for you. He's putting up new wallpaper and buying a new bed. Won't that be nice?"

Brenda looked sad. "I liked my old room," she said. "Will God know I have a new room? Will He hear me pray in my new bed?"

"Oh, yes," said Aunt Jill. "God took care of Uncle Dave and me when we moved to this apartment. He will take care of you, too."

Just then Uncle Dave came in. He asked, "Who wants to go to the ice-cream shop?"

"I do," said Brenda. "And God will take care of us all the way."

PRAYER
Dear God, help me remember You are with me wherever I am.

A BIBLE VERSE TO REMEMBER

My God will meet all your needs according to his glorious riches in Christ Jesus. PHILIPPIANS 4:19

PARENTS: As you run errands, ask your child who is with you in each place—at the post office, at the store, in the library, etc. Say together, "God is with us!"

Jesus Teaches Us to Obey
MATTHEW 7:24-29

Jesus told His friends many stories. One day He told them this story about obeying God's Word:

Once there were two men who built new houses. One man was wise. He looked for just the right place to build his house. He built his house on a big, strong rock.

The other man was not smart. He was foolish. He built his house on sand. Sand is not a good place to build a house.

Soon after the houses were finished, it rained very hard! Thunder boomed and lightning flashed. Water splashed around the houses.

The wise man's house that was built on rock wasn't hurt at all. But the foolish man's house that was built on sand fell down with a CRASH!

Jesus said that people who obey God's Word are like the wise man. And people who don't obey God's Word are like the foolish man.

PRAYER
Dear God, please help me to obey Your Word just as the
wise man did.

A BIBLE VERSE TO REMEMBER
"If you love me, you will obey what I command."   JOHN 14:15

The Big Mess
MATTHEW 7:24-29

Brenda ate dinner with Aunt Jill. Then she looked for something quiet to do. She decided to give her doll a bath in the sink. That was quiet.

Brenda did not ask Aunt Jill. She put her doll in the sink and turned on the water. Up the water came, up toward the edge of the sink. "No more water," said Brenda, but she could not turn it off.

The water came over the edge of the sink and spilled out on the floor. Then Aunt Jill came in.

Aunt Jill said, "Oh, Brenda, what a mess. Let's clean it up." She brought sponges, and they wiped the floor.

"Do you still love me?" asked Brenda. "Does Jesus love me?"

"We both do," said Aunt Jill. And she gave Brenda a hug.

PRAYER
Thank You, Jesus, for loving me even when I do wrong things.

A BIBLE VERSE TO REMEMBER
"If you love me, you will obey what I command."   JOHN 14:15

PARENTS: Tell a story about something you should not have done as a child and how your parents handled it. Then reassure your child that your love—and Jesus' love—is there whether the child is being "wise" or "foolish."

Down Through the Roof
MARK 2:1-12

One day, Jesus was in a house telling people about God. Four men came to the house. They were carrying their friend who was sick and couldn't walk. The men wanted to see Jesus. They knew He could make their friend well.

But they couldn't even get to the door. So many people wanted to hear Jesus that the crowd filled the house and the doorway.

The four men took their friend up to the flat roof of the house. They made a hole in the roof. Then they tied strong ropes on the man's bed and let him down through the hole. Soon he was right in front of Jesus.

Jesus loved the man and wanted to help him. He said to the sick man, "Get up off your bed and walk."

The man got up! Jesus had made him well.

Everyone was surprised. "We have never seen anything like this!" they said. They thought Jesus was wonderful.

PRAYER
Dear Jesus, I know You are God's Son and You can do wonderful things!

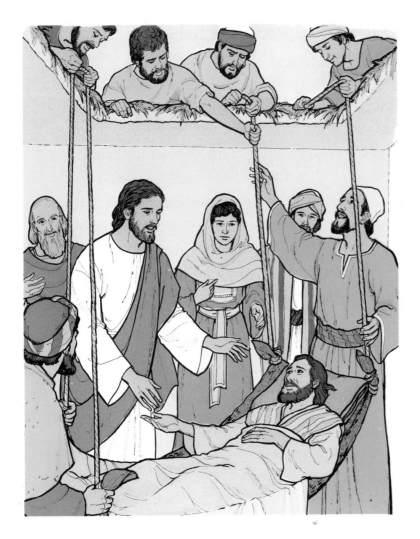

It's Nice to Have Friends
MARK 2:1-12

Brenda had a cold. Her nose was red and sniffily. But worst of all, Brenda couldn't spend the day with Mrs. Ferguson, her baby-sitter.

Mother said, "I called Mrs. Ferguson. She said she hopes you'll get better soon. She will have the children pray for you."

Brenda smiled, but she still felt a little lonely—especially when she thought of the banana muffins Mrs. Ferguson was baking that day.

Later, the doorbell woke Brenda up. Mr. Ferguson stood on the steps with get-well cards from all the children and Mrs. Ferguson. He also had a basket of banana muffins! Brenda said to her mother, "It's nice to have good friends, especially when you're sick!"

PRAYER
Dear Jesus, thank You for taking good care of me when I get sick.

A BIBLE VERSE TO REMEMBER
They praised God, saying, "We have never seen anything like this!"

MARK 2:12B

PARENTS: Have your child color a picture. Put it in a get-well card and together send it to a sick or shut-in friend. Pray with your child for this friend.

Jesus Chooses a Helper
MATTHEW 9:9-13

Matthew's job was to take money from the people to give to the king. One day, Jesus walked by. He said to Matthew, "Follow Me."

Matthew got up and followed Jesus. He wanted to be Jesus' helper.

"Come and eat supper with me," Matthew said to Jesus. Matthew asked his friends to eat with them, too. His friends did bad things, but Matthew wanted them to meet Jesus.

Some important people said to Jesus' helpers, "Why is Jesus eating with Matthew and his bad friends?"

Jesus heard them and said, "Matthew and his friends need me. I can help Matthew and his friends be good."

Jesus didn't like the bad things Matthew and his friends did, but Jesus loved them. He wanted them to stop doing bad things and do good things instead. He knew Matthew could be a good helper.

Jesus loves everyone. He wants everyone to love Him, too.

PRAYER
Dear Jesus, I am sorry for the bad things I do. I want to be Your helper and do good things.

A BIBLE VERSE TO REMEMBER

. . . Since God so loved us, we also ought to love one another.   I JOHN 4:11

The Best Gift
MATTHEW 9:9-13

Michael and his mother bought a Bible picture book for cousin Sara. She hurt her knee and could not walk. Michael ran up to Sara's room.

"Here's a present!" Michael said.

Cousin Sara tore open the pretty paper. "A book," she said, "with lots of pictures. I like books, but I can't read the words."

Michael couldn't read, either, but he knew these stories. They looked at each picture, and Michael told Sara the stories.

"This is when baby Jesus was born," said Michael. "And here is Jesus when He grew up. He is helping people."

Michael liked being Jesus' helper and telling Sara stories about Jesus.

PRAYER
Dear Jesus, I want to be Your helper and tell someone
about You.

A BIBLE VERSE TO REMEMBER

. . . Since God so loved us, we also ought to love one another.

I JOHN 4:11

PARENTS: *Help your child to think of ways he can be Jesus' helper. Perhaps he can tell his favorite Bible stories to a friend as they look at the pictures in this book.*

Jesus Makes a Sick Man Well
JOHN 5:1-9

Jesus saw many sick people by a big pool of water. He stopped by one man who was lying there on his bed mat. Jesus knew that the man had been sick for a long time.

Jesus looked down at the sick man. "Would you like to get well?" Jesus asked him.

The sick man looked up at Jesus and said, "Sir, I want to be well, but there is no one who can help me."

But Jesus could help the man. Jesus is God's Son. He can do anything.

Jesus said to the man, "Get up. Pick up your bed mat and walk!"

And all at once, the man got well. He stood up. He picked up his bed mat. And he began to walk. How wonderful the man must have felt!

No matter how busy Jesus was, He helped people who needed Him.

PRAYER
Thank You, Jesus, that You always have time to help me.

A BIBLE VERSE TO REMEMBER

. . . Let us do good to all people.

GALATIANS 6:10B

Good Helpers
JOHN 5:1-9

Michael and his mother were shopping at the mall. Sherri and Shawna and their mother were shopping, too.

Sherri and Shawna saw Michael. They said, "We're going for ice cream. Can you come with us?"

Michael and his mother liked that idea. So they followed the twins and their mother to the ice-cream shop. Mr. Ferguson was having ice cream there. His arm was broken and he had it in a sling.

Michael said, "Does your arm hurt, Mr. Ferguson?"

Mr. Ferguson said, "My broken arm doesn't hurt. But my other arm hurts from carrying my packages."

Michael said, "Don't worry, Mr. Ferguson. We can help by carrying your packages." And that's just what Michael and Sherri and Shawna did.

PRAYER
Dear Jesus, I want to help people, just like You do!

A BIBLE VERSE TO REMEMBER

. . . Let us do good to all people.   GALATIANS 6:10B

PARENTS: Help your child notice others who need them when you are away from home. Suggest that your child open the door for a mother carrying a baby or pick up an item someone has dropped. When your child helps, remind him that he is doing good, just as the Bible verse says to do.

Jesus Teaches Us How to Be Happy
MARK 12:28-34

One day a teacher asked Jesus a question: "What is the one thing God wants us to do most of all?"

Jesus answered, "Love God with all of your heart. That is the most important thing to do."

The man listened carefully and nodded his head. He knew Jesus was right.

Jesus spoke again. "There is something else you should do that is very important. You should love other people, too."

The man nodded his head. He smiled at Jesus. "Yes," he said. "You are right. These are the best things for us to do. We should love God and love other people. That is more important than anything else!"

Jesus said, "God is happy when we do these things, and we are happy, too."

PRAYER
Dear God, help me to love You most of all.

*A BIBLE VERSE
TO REMEMBER*
*"Love the Lord
your God with all
your heart . . ."*
MARK 12:30A

Carlos Shows Love
MARK 12:28-34

After Sunday school, Michael was hungry. But Michael's father and Carlos's father talked and talked. Michael climbed into his car seat. But his father still talked and talked.

Michael knew he had to fasten his seat belt. He pulled the belt. He pulled again. The belt was stuck.

Carlos came to the car. "Help," said Michael. "My seat belt is stuck." Carlos twisted the seat belt and pulled. Click! Michael was buckled. "Thanks, Carlos," Michael said. "Jesus must have sent you to help."

"Yes," said Carlos. "And guess what! I'm going to your house for lunch." Then he climbed into the car next to Michael to wait for their fathers.

PRAYER
Dear God, please show me how to love people by helping them.

54

A BIBLE VERSE TO REMEMBER

"Love the Lord your God with all your heart . . ."   MARK 12:30A

PARENTS: As you help your child with seat belts or shoelaces, tell him that you are showing your love for him by helping him. Talk about ways he can show his love for his friends, as Carlos did for Michael.

A Man Is Kind
LUKE 10:25-37

One day Jesus told this story: While a man was traveling down a road, some bad men stopped him. They took his clothes and money. Then they beat him up and left him.

The man was hurt and needed help. He saw someone coming down the road. But the man coming down the road walked on by.

The man felt even worse. He hurt so much! Soon, he saw another man coming. But that man crossed the road and didn't stop to help.

Finally another man came along. He was from a country called Samaria. The man who was hurt didn't think this man would stop.

But the man from Samaria did stop. He put medicine and bandages on the man's sores. Then he took him to an inn and paid for a place for the hurt man to stay.

The man felt better. The man from Samaria saved his life!

When Jesus finished the story He said, "You should be kind to everyone, just as the man from Samaria was kind."

PRAYER
Dear Jesus, thank You for showing me how to be kind to people.

Being Kind to Friends
LUKE 10:25-37

Brenda's family had invited Carlos and his family for supper. When supper was almost over, someone knocked on the door. It was Mrs. Lee and her son Scott. Mrs. Lee said, "My car broke down. May I use the phone to call for help?"

"Yes," said Brenda's mother.

Carlos's father said, "Maybe we can fix it."

Brenda's mother poured tea for the mothers while the fathers went to fix the car.

Brenda watched her mother be kind to Mrs. Lee. Brenda wanted to be kind to Scott, too. "Do you want some lemonade?" she asked.

"Sure," said Scott.

Brenda's mother helped pour lemonade for Scott and Carlos and Brenda. By the time the fathers had fixed the car, all the children were good friends.

PRAYER
Dear Jesus, please help me to be kind to people.

A BIBLE VERSE TO REMEMBER

Be kind and loving to each other. EPHESIANS 4:32A (ICB)

PARENTS: Use small paper lunch bags to help your child make puppets of the injured man, the passersby, and the Samaritan. With crayons or markers, draw faces on the bottom of the bags and clothing on the side of the bags. Then use the puppets to act out the story of the kind Samaritan. Emphasize how the Samaritan was kind to someone he didn't even know.

One Lost Sheep
LUKE 15:1-7

Jesus told this story about a shepherd who had one hundred sheep.

The shepherd took good care of his sheep. He made sure nothing could hurt them and that they found enough grass to eat and water to drink. At night he kept them safe in a sheep pen where no wild animals could hurt them.

One day a little sheep wandered off from the other sheep. As it was running and jumping, the sheep got its foot caught in a bush.

When night came, the shepherd took his sheep to the pen to sleep. But one sheep was missing! The shepherd went back to the field to find his little sheep. He looked and looked. At last he found the lost sheep. He untangled its foot from the bush and carried it back to the other sheep.

The shepherd was happy. He called to his friends, "Be happy with me! My little sheep was lost, but now I have found it."

PRAYER
Thank You, Jesus, that I am Your little sheep.

A BIBLE VERSE TO REMEMBER

The Lord is my shepherd. PSALM 23:1A

Special and Different
LUKE 15:1-7

Sherri and Shawna were visiting Grandma and Grandpa. Grandma said, "Sherri—I mean Shawna—come put your shoes on. Shawna—I mean Sherri—put on your coat. Grandpa will take you both for a walk."

Sherri said, "Grandpa, do you know if I am Sherri or Shawna?"

Grandpa said, "You are Sherri."

Shawna said, "I wish I was special and different from everybody else."

Grandpa said, "I think you are both very special and different. Sherri, do you like green beans?"

"Yuk," said Sherri.

"I love green beans," said Shawna.

"That's one way you are different," said Grandpa. "You each like different foods. Jesus knows even more ways that you are different. Each of His little lambs is very, very special to Him."

PRAYER
Dear Jesus, thank You that I am special to You.

A BIBLE VERSE TO REMEMBER

The Lord is my shepherd. PSALM 23:1A

PARENTS: Encourage your child to act like a shepherd as he cares for his stuffed animals and remind him that Jesus is his shepherd. Sing these words to the tune of "The Farmer in the Dell": Oh, Jesus cares for me; oh, Jesus cares for me. He will help me when I'm scared; oh, Jesus cares for me.

The Day Zacchaeus Met Jesus
LUKE 19:1-10

"Jesus is coming!" people shouted. Zacchaeus looked, but He couldn't see Jesus. He was short, and tall people were in his way. So Zacchaeus climbed a sycamore tree. Then he saw Jesus coming down the road.

Zacchaeus's job was to collect money from people and send it to the king for them. Sometimes Zacchaeus took more money than he should have, and he kept it.

As Jesus came nearer, He saw Zacchaeus in the tree. "Come down," Jesus called to him. "I want to have dinner at your house." Zacchaeus came down in a hurry. How glad he was to take Jesus to his house!

Zacchaeus started thinking about all the bad things he had done. He told Jesus he was sorry for taking money from people. "I will give half my money to poor people. If I have taken too much money from people, I will give it back—and more."

Jesus was glad Zacchaeus was sorry for doing wrong things. And Zacchaeus was happy when he did what Jesus wanted him to do.

PRAYER

Dear Jesus, I am sorry for the wrong things I have done today.

The Broken Vase
LUKE 19:1-10

There was a rule at Michael's house that said: No running inside. But Michael said to Brenda, "You can't catch me!"

Brenda chased Michael until—CRASH! A vase fell down and broke.

Michael's mother hurried in. Michael said, "We were running and the vase broke. We're sorry."

Michael's mother helped the children pray. They said, "Dear Jesus, we know You want us to obey. We are sorry. We love You. Amen."

Then Michael's mother hugged them. She said, "Jesus forgives you, and so do I."

Brenda got the dustpan. Michael got the broom. And they helped clean up.

PRAYER
Thank You, Jesus, for forgiving me when I do something bad.

A BIBLE VERSE TO REMEMBER

But if we confess our sins to him, he can be depended on to forgive us and to cleanse us from every wrong.

I JOHN 1:9A (*The Illustrated Bible*, TLB)

PARENTS: Scoldings are not fun, but you can pray for Jesus' love and patience. Set aside a special place where you can help your child pray for forgiveness and get a forgiving hug.

Angels Tell That Jesus Is Alive
LUKE 24:1-12

Jesus' friends were sad because Jesus was dead. His friends buried Him in a cave called a tomb.

Very early one morning, some women who knew Jesus went to His tomb. They wanted to put sweet-smelling spices on Jesus' body. As they walked along, they wondered how they would move the big stone that was in front of the tomb's door.

But when they got to the tomb, the stone was rolled away from the door. The women went inside, but they didn't see Jesus' body. They saw two shining angels. "Why are you looking for Jesus here?" the angels asked. "He isn't dead anymore. He is alive again, just as He said He would be."

How happy they were! Jesus was alive again. He would be with them again. The women ran off to tell Jesus' helpers the happy news.

PRAYER
Dear Jesus, I am so happy You are alive!

A BIBLE VERSE TO REMEMBER

"He is not here; he has risen!"

LUKE 24:6A

The Best Secret
LUKE 24:1-12

On Easter morning, Miss Karen whispered a secret to each person in her Sunday school class. Then Miss Karen said, "Let's tell our secret out loud."

Everyone shouted, "Jesus is alive!"

"I want to tell everyone the secret," said Michael.

Miss Karen said, "Here are some cards that say 'Jesus is alive.' We can use them to tell everyone." So the children folded the cards and colored them.

"Who should we give them to?" asked Miss Karen.

"Pastor Russell," said Brenda.

"One for everybody," said Carlos.

So the children went to each class in church and left a card. At each room they told their secret, "Jesus is alive!" Everyone liked the cards. They all thought it was the best secret they had ever heard.

PRAYER
Dear Jesus, I want to tell EVERYBODY that You are alive!

A BIBLE VERSE TO REMEMBER

"He is not here; he has risen!"   LUKE 24:6A

*PARENTS: Angels are usually associated with Christmas. But why not
help your child make angel-shaped cookies this week? As you work
together, talk about the wonderful message the two angels gave the
women at the tomb.*

Jesus' Helpers Know He Is Alive
JOHN 20:19-29

Thomas had been one of Jesus' helpers. He was sad when Jesus died!

One day, Jesus' other helpers ran to see Thomas. "If only you had been with us last night, Thomas. We were upstairs and had locked the doors. Suddenly, Jesus was standing right in the room with us!"

"I don't believe you," Thomas said. "Jesus died. How can He be alive again? I won't believe it unless I can see and touch Him."

A week later Jesus' helpers were in the same upstairs room with the doors locked. Now Thomas was with them. Suddenly, Jesus was there! He said to everyone, "May peace be with you."

Then He said, "Come here, Thomas. Touch Me."

Thomas cried, "My Lord and my God!"

Jesus said, "Thomas, you believe because you see Me. You are happy. Some people will believe I am alive even though they have never seen Me. They will be very happy because they'll know I am always with them."

PRAYER

Dear Jesus, I haven't seen You, but I know You are always with me.

A BIBLE VERSE TO REMEMBER
God has said, "I will never leave you; I will never forget you."
HEBREWS 13:5B (ICB)

Michael's Postcard
JOHN 20:19-29

Michael had a picture postcard of a mountain. Miss Karen read the card. She read, "Dear Michael, I like living here. Love, Grandma."

Michael said, "My grandma moved a long way from here. I don't get to see her anymore."

"Jesus went away, too," said Carlos. "I remember."

"Did Jesus move to the mountains with Michael's grandma?" asked Brenda.

Miss Karen said, "After Jesus came back to life and talked with His helpers, He went to be with God in heaven."

"If Jesus sent us a postcard from heaven, would it take a lot of stamps?" asked Carlos.

Miss Karen said, "Jesus doesn't need to send postcards, because even though He is in heaven, He is with us here, too. He is with us wherever we go, and He cares about everything we do."

PRAYER
Dear Jesus, I'm glad You are with me right now and You know what I'm doing!

A BIBLE VERSE TO REMEMBER

God has said, "I will never leave you; I will never forget you."
HEBREWS 13:5B (ICB)

PARENTS: Take a walk with your child on a windy day. Point out that he cannot see the wind, but he can see how the wind makes things move. Remind your child that Jesus is with us every day even though we can't see Him.

Jesus' Friends Work Together
ACTS 4:32-37; 6:7

After Jesus went back to heaven, Jesus' friends wanted to help each other. They began to live together. They brought all their things together and divided them. That way everyone had enough food and clothes and money. Jesus' friends were happy to share their things. They knew that would make their friend Jesus happy.

Jesus' friends told other people about Jesus. Lots of people believed in Him. And lots of people came to live with Jesus' friends. They were like one big family living together.

How happy Jesus' friends were that they could work and share together. How happy they were to tell people about their special friend Jesus.

PRAYER
Dear Jesus, I love to tell people about You, my special friend.

A BIBLE VERSE TO REMEMBER
"You are my friends if you do what I command."   JOHN 15:14

Brenda, the 'Hello' Friend
ACTS 4:32-37; 6:7

One Sunday Peter came to Sunday school for the first time. Mrs. Lee picked Brenda to be a "hello" friend for Peter.

First Brenda and Peter went to where Mrs. Lee was helping the children make a church building out of a big box. Brenda crawled inside the box and said, "Come on, Peter. You can play, too."

Next Brenda and Peter went to the music center where they sang a song with Miss Karen about the church family.

Then Pastor Russell came. Brenda said, "Peter is new."

Pastor Russell said, "How do you like our Sunday school, Peter?"

Peter smiled at Brenda and said, "I like it a *lot!*"

PRAYER
Dear Jesus, please help me to be a "hello" friend when I
meet someone new.

78

A BIBLE VERSE TO REMEMBER
"You are my friends if you do what I command."   JOHN 15:14

PARENTS: Plan a friendly gesture with your preschooler. Take an elderly person grocery shopping. Invite a neighbor child to Sunday school. Show your child by your actions how to be a friend.

If you and your children enjoyed reading *My First Book of Bible Devotions*, you'll want the companion book *My Little Bible Picture Book*, available at your local Christian bookstore.

My Little Bible Picture Book is just right for a child's first look at the Bible, introducing many stories and people—from Creation to the early church.